WASHINGTON

The Spirit of the Land

Text by LYNDA V. MAPES

Photography by TERRY DONNELLY *and* MARY LIZ AUSTIN

Foreword by TIM PALMER

VOYAGEUR PRESS

page one
Yellow vine maples on a moss-covered, rocky hillside, Cascade River canyon, North Cascades National Park

pages two–three
Silver light at dusk playing on the tide pools and sea stacks of Ruby Beach, Olympic National Park

Edited by Todd R. Berger
Designed by Kristy Tucker
Printed in Hong Kong

99   00   01   02   03   5   4   3   2   1

Library of Congress Cataloging-in-Publication Data

Mapes, Lynda V., 1959—
    Washington : the spirit of the land / text by Lynda Mapes ; photography by Terry Donnelly and Mary Liz Austin.
        p. cm.
    Includes bibliographical references (p. 140–142).
    ISBN 0-89658-415-1
    1. Washington (State)—Description and travel. 2. Washington (State) Pictorial works. 3. Landscape—Washington (State) Pictorial works. 4. Natural history—Washington (State). I. Title.
F895.M37 1999
917.97—dc21   99-14767
                             CIP

Distributed in Canada by Raincoast Books,
8680 Cambie Street, Vancouver, B.C. V6P 6M9

Published by Voyageur Press, Inc.
123 North Second Street, P.O. Box 338, Stillwater, MN 55082 U.S.A.
651-430-2210, fax 651-430-2211

Educators, fundraisers, premium and gift buyers, publicists, and marketing managers: Looking for creative products and new sales ideas? Voyageur Press books are available at special discounts when purchased in quantities, and special editions can be created to your specifications. For details contact the marketing department at 800-888-9653.

The Nisqually River valley at sunset,
Mount Rainier National Park

DEDICATION

To the people of Washington who have worked to preserve and protect these beautiful places.

AUTHOR'S ACKNOWLEDGMENTS

A book like this relies on the knowledge and assistance of many people. In particular, I would like to thank: Jon Riedel, park geologist of North Cascades National Park, who spent many hours explaining the geology of the park to me and provided helpful suggestions on the manuscript; Robert Flores, project leader, and Randy Hill, wildlife biologist with the U.S. Fish and Wildlife Service, who taught me about the wonderful sagebrush country at the Columbia National Wildlife Refuge in Othello; Dana Illo, who introduced me to the Fern Cove Sanctuary on Vashon Island and told me the story of its preservation; and Ray Lasmanis, state geologist with the Washington Department of Natural Resources, who helped explain the fascinating geologic story behind Washington's land forms.

For the account of the eruption of Mount St. Helens, I am indebted to *Northwest Exposures: A Geologic Story of the Northwest* by David Alt and Donald Hyndman.

Finally, I thank my husband, Zack Krieger, for his patience during many nights, weekends, and "vacations" spent in the field and at the keyboard.

PHOTOGRAPHERS' ACKNOWLEDGMENTS

We would like to thank Bruce Haulman for generously sharing his time on the trawler *Vashona* and for his solid nautical skills, which provided us with access to the more remote waters of Puget Sound and the San Juan Islands. Our great appreciation is also due to Tammie Grabill of High Valley Llama Treks for her guiding expertise and loving llamas who dutifully packed our equipment deep into the valleys of North Cascades National Park. Finally, we are very grateful to Ruth Anderson who capably manages our office while we are out searching for those perfect moments in nature.

pages eight–nine
An alder extending its branches over the blue waters of Lake Crescent, Olympic National Park

Quaking aspens on the edge of a grassy meadow, Wenatchee National Forest

CONTENTS

FOREWORD BY TIM PALMER   10

INTRODUCTION   12

CHAPTER 1   EARTH   18

CHAPTER 2   AIR   42

CHAPTER 3   FIRE   62

CHAPTER 4   WATER   90

CHAPTER 5   SPIRIT   118

CONCLUSION   138

BIBLIOGRAPHY   140

PHOTO CREDITS   143

ABOUT THE AUTHOR
AND PHOTOGRAPHERS   144

FOREWORD

by Tim Palmer

STRAIGHT AHEAD, ABOVE my desk in a drab college dormitory room, a picture of Mount Rainier whispered to me softly, seductively, constantly. I had clipped it out of a tourist brochure. From my vantage point three thousand miles away, the celestial quality of the icy volcano hardly seemed possible. Yet it was. I knew it was, because the photograph proved that this place existed. The image of blue, green, white, and brown gave me nothing less than hope for something wonderful awaiting me.

Thus primed, I flew west in June. I had scored a summer job in a national park. As my plane neared Seattle, clouds sealed off the entire Northwest from my tiny window view, but then, as the drone of the plane grew deeper, as we dropped elevation by ear-popping degrees, as we banked slightly to the left, *It* appeared. The upper half of the mountain—already familiar to me—emerged from the cloud blanket and reached toward heaven, its summit every bit as high as we were, and my thrill could not be described. Massive, corniced in white, gleaming in golden sun above the oceanic cloudmass below, Rainier pulled on me, as God-like as anything my youthful heart could imagine.

So it is in the great state of Washington. Longing to know it all, I started in the northwest corner by backpacking along the stellar coast of the Olympic Peninsula, a wildness of ocean shore, craggy headland, and ancient forest. During the following years I wandered my way across to the far southeastern corner of the state. I saw examples of everything people do to land and water.

In this journey from one corner of the state to the other, from pure nature to the unnecessary death of nature, I realized two things. First, our land survives in abundant beauty. Second, our response to all that abundance and all that beauty ranges from fully respectful stewardship to pitifully shortsighted exploitation. Only by knowing what is here—by seeing the perfection in it, understanding the value of it, sensing the enchantment possible with it—can we advance the stewardship and cut the exploitative losses.

With pictures such as the one of Mount Rainier that stirred me so many years ago, and with words that help us to understand the gift of good land to all Washingtonians, this book can help us to know the wonders of our country. Mary Liz Austin, Terry Donnelly, and Lynda Mapes have opened a window through which all of us might see this very special place and thereby know it and grow more committed to caring for it well.

Tim Palmer is the author of The Columbia, The Heart of America, Lifelines, *and other books.*

Springtime flow of the Palouse River, Palouse Falls State Park

INTRODUCTION

I F YOU ARE lucky, there is a landscape you love to visit and look after. It is where you go to reconnect to your better self, to find the quiet that is the music of nature.

Here in Washington, there are countless landscapes that offer this sense of place, that tell us we are home. These touchstones of the natural world keep us whole. They are places to contemplate where we have been and where we ought to go. They are, most preciously, quiet places.

There is a spirit of the land that abides. We feel it when we are in these landscapes, and carry it in our heart when we leave.

Washington is generous that way.

The diversity of the landscapes of Washington amazes me. Rain-swept forests, whitewater rivers, and glaciated mountains give way to sculpted towers of basalt and arid sagebrush steppes.

Yet there is great continuity between these landscapes, no matter how different they appear.

Salmon travel the vast watershed of the Columbia River, swimming from the furthest inland desert reaches of the state to the five-mile-wide river mouth, more than three hundred miles distant to the sea. These noble fish swim back again to their home river, knitting miles of habitat and all of us together with the bright silver flash of their lives.

Watersheds link mountains to glacial meltwater streams and rivers that rush headlong to the sea. Water is Washington's great gift. It gives us the whisper of rain, the music of waterfalls, the lifeblood of rivers and booming tides.

The native people, here thousands of years before Washington was a state, have a wealth of stories of the land that nurtured, inspired, and taught them. Each tribe and each family has its own stories, and they are all different. But there are common themes, including the importance of care and respect for the natural world. And they teach that greed, or wasting what is given the People, whether it is salmon or pure water, is wrong.

These myths also are imbued with a sense of living in a spirit of the land.

Many native people believe the natural world is alive with spirit helpers who, if sought and respected, offer protection, special powers, guidance, sustenance, and direction. These spirit helpers live in animals, the woods, the mountains, the water, everywhere that nature is.

We are tied as closely to nature today and its essential elements of earth, air, fire, and water as the First People. And the spirit helpers that guide their lives are alive in the beauty of the natural world that inspires, consoles, and counsels us. In Washington, where a spirit of wild nature still breathes free, these essential elements are richly abundant in the many gifts of the landscape.

Earth is the fantastic geologic stories the coulees, Channeled Scablands,

Picture Lake with evening clouds and reflection of Mount Shuksan, Mount Baker–Snoqualmie National Forest

Lupine, arrowleaf balsam root, and sage below the cliffs of the Lower Grand Coulee, North Columbia Basin Wildlife Area

volcanoes, and glaciers have to tell. It is the fructifying funk of Washington's mossy rain forests, and the grandeur of gigantic, old-growth trees.

Water is the life-giving abundance that defines much of this state, whether it's the twelve feet of rain that soak temperate rain forests; the salmon streams; the salt water; or the hydrologic cycle of clouds, precipitation, and rivers flowing to the Pacific and back up to the sky.

Fire is the glow of autumn foliage and raging sunsets, the blaze in sunlit icy branches and frosted grass, the steam from volcanoes, and the relentless heat that bakes the deserts.

Air is Washington's ever-changing atmosphere, which is pellucid east of the mountains and a fantastic pageant of cloud banks, mist, fog, and dew to the west.

And finally, spirit is the gift of the landscape. The mystery of spectral fog, the inspiration of shining glaciers, the quiet of the deep forest. The spaciousness of the sagebrush steppes and the music of streams. The poetry of wildflowers, the glory of shining autumn leaves, and the counsel of the great ocean.

Salt marsh grasses near Leadbetter Point on Willapa Bay, Willapa National Wildlife Refuge

These landscapes are deeply healing. To scoop butter clams from clean sand alongside the lapping tidewater and drink clam nectar under the stars is to connect with an ancient memory of living from the abundance of the land. So is feeling the ache of a glacier-cold, free-flowing river on the fingers. So is kicking through fragrant sagebrush, and watching the play of sunlight across the basalt sculptures of the Channeled Scablands, with the wind in your ears.

We need the taste, feel, perfume, beauty, and music of wild nature. We need it as surely as we do clean water and clean air.

In Washington, we are lucky. We are nurtured and renewed by these gifts, and by the spirit of the land.

Gray skies over Perfection Lake, Enchantment Lakes, Alpine Lakes Wilderness Area, Wenatchee National Forest

Blue-pod lupine blooming near Sunbeam Creek, Mount Rainier National Park

CHAPTER 1

EARTH

Morning light on snow-covered peaks of Johannesburg
Mountain at Cascade Pass, North Cascades
National Park

L ISTEN TO WASHINGTON's ancient ones: the glaciers that mantle the mountains, the old-growth forests, the basalt sculptures carved by prehistoric floodwaters.

They tell the story of the birth and evolution of this varied and beautiful land.

The Cascade and Olympic Mountains are testimony to the relentless forces of nature that created the high country and shape it still. The mountains are laced with waterfalls, craggy with steep cliffs and hanging glaciers, and full of the wild sound of cracking ice and avalanches.

Drop down to western Washington's forested lowlands and you will encounter cathedral-like groves of old-growth trees, and the green and padded realm of the temperate rain forests, hung with swags of moss.

Cross the Cascade Mountains, and suddenly all that green changes to a desert palette of baking basalt rock in hues of bronze, brown, black, and mauve. In central Washington, golden tufts of bunch grass are bleached to straw, and dry washes of gravel and talus form a forbidding land.

In central Washington and further east, the rugged beauty of the Channeled Scablands is softened by brilliant wildflowers come spring, and the silver green of sagebrush year round.

In southeast Washington, the angular cliffs and polygons of basalt give way to the soft, rolling curves of the Palouse country, where a deep topsoil called loess, a gift of winds and glaciers, nourishes some of the richest crop land in the country.

These are the varied faces of Washington's landscape, the many sculptures formed from the earth.

Common sunflowers and basalt boulders backlit by morning sun with green hills descending into the Snake River valley, Asotin County

The San Juans are made largely of sandstone, and the long afternoon light on their sheer sides is a poem of rose, orange, and warm sandy tones.

Kayaking by these sandstone cliffs is sweetened by the refraction of the music of the water off the sheer, bare rock. I also love the way the sandstone holds the heat of the sun and thrusts it back at you over the cold salt water.

The San Juans are actually the drowned foothills of the North Cascades, sculpted by glaciers. Identical fossils of marine life appear in both the North Cascades and the San Juans, geologists say. These foothills, which today show only their tips, were buried deep under an ice lobe that extended from Canada all the way down into the south Puget Sound area. These glaciers deeply cut and carved the land, later covered by salt water. The uneven terrain below the water makes for treacherous currents today, as the tide sucks through deep-cut channels, canyons, and funnels of rock below the surface.

Any safe kayaking adventure in the San Juans begins with careful consideration of the tide chart. Nature makes the rules. I like that.

PACIFIC MADRONE

The marvelous Pacific madrone is always up to something, whether it's shedding great peels of colorful bark; showing off its vivid, bare wood; or bursting forth in sweet-scented white flowers that give way to blazing red berries.

Pacific madrone is the tallest North American evergreen broadleaf tree and can become huge, towering to eighty feet in height. It is the largest of a family of plants that includes azaleas, blueberries, heathers, salal, and rhododendron.

Madrones can be extremely long-lived, lasting 200 to 250 years. They tolerate dry and rocky soil other trees shun, but love the coast best. Madrones are seldom found far from salt water.

Madrones shed their shiny, green leaves all year long. This constant grooming allows the tree to maintain a thick glossy mantle of green even in deep winter.

Also called arbutus, madrones are creatures of the sun. Their trunks will run fully horizontal like a vine along the forest floor, or twist through dark conifer bows to reach the light.

But it is the bark that truly sets this tree apart. As the tree grows, the bark breaks into scales, exposing the inner bark and bare wood beneath. Long peels of shed bark will hang from the tree and gather beneath it, dry and brick red as pottery shards. In the rain, where the bare wood shows through, it shines smooth and sleek as wet skin.

In the dark months of winter, madrone berries glow in the gloom. When the sun breaks out, flocks of robins cover madrone trees, gobbling the brilliant red fruits. I love the sound of dozens of them rustling in the leaves and their soft, birdy conversation.

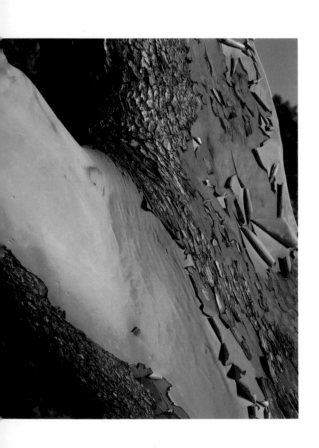

The trunk of an old Pacific madrone with peeling red bark, Stuart Island, San Juan Islands

Pacific madrone and Douglas fir forest on white cliffs at Turn Point, Stuart Island, San Juan Islands

The red alder or Oregon alder is one of our few big deciduous citizens, towering as much as 120 feet and spreading a generous, soft foliage above the forest floor. Red alder commonly grows in groups, each tree leaning toward the other in picturesque conversation.

To me, the soft, grayish white bark of this tree is its loveliest feature. A paving of lichen over their trunks is what makes the trees look white. In the dark conifer forests, the trunks have a ghostly glow. Moss will often patch the bark in shaggy hanks on its north and west sides, giving it a venerable beard.

In the spring, alder lifts my spirits. After months of gray, wet weather, I will notice a pinkish glow in the trees. The haze of color is from new alder buds, and I know that soon lettuce-green leaves will dapple the soft spring light.

WESTERN RED CEDAR

In this dense gloom, the elders of Washington's forests reside.

The Grove of the Patriarchs is a ninety-four-acre forest of ancient trees including one thousand-year-old western red cedars that have reached heights of nearly three hundred feet and diameters of eight feet.

Cedars live longer than other conifers because they resist rot and insect attack. They also have a wide base that forms a natural buttress and helps them withstand high winds.

The ancient giants in this grove were spared from fire because they grow on an island in the Ohanapecosh River. The river's periodic floods also nourish the soil. Ideal growing conditions in this grove have nurtured some of the largest trees in the country. They have been protected from logging since the creation of Mount Rainier National Park in 1899.

Western red cedar, scientists say, has graced Washington forests for about five thousand years. This glorious tree, with its fragrant, spicy branches, is braided into the lives of Washington tribes.

The Quinault, Makah, Shoalwater, Hoh, and other coastal tribes have relied on cedar for millennia. They carved cedar, a soft and easily worked wood, into masks, household boxes, bowls, and rattles. They also built communal homes called longhouses from great cedar planks lashed together with bark.

Weavers fashioned blankets and clothing from twisted twine or cord of cedar bark fiber, and they also wove the bark into hats and shawls. Cordage from cedar fibers was made into dip nets for salmon fishing and split cedar bark was woven into bags and baskets.

While cedar was important to every western Washington tribe, coastal tribes depended on it. Some women on the Makah reservation in the far northwestern corner of the state still know how to weave cedar bark so tightly it looks like cloth.

Stand of western red cedar trunks with decomposing western hemlock, Grove of the Patriarchs, Mount Rainier National Park

Grove of red alder in the Sol Duc
River valley, Olympic National Park

Glaciers and snowfields on the north
face of Mount Adams, from Takhlakh
Lake, Gifford Pinchot National Forest

Glaciers are the sculptors of the earth, grinding, polishing, pushing, and shoving the landscape to their slow-moving whim.

Mount Adams, 12,307 feet high, is the second-highest in the Cascade Range, after Rainier. Adams also holds the second-largest glacier in the Cascade Range, the Klickitat, on its east side.

The high peaks, cold temperatures, and moisture-laden Pacific winds provide the perfect recipe for glacier formation. When snow falls and does not melt away for years, glaciers are born. The weight of new snow compresses existing snowpack to ice. As the weight increases, ice underneath the glacier becomes plastic and starts to flow. The glacier moves.

As it does so, the glacier's enormous weight grinds and saws at the earth and transports huge stones plucked from solid bedrock. Geologists call these rocks, transported from distant locations, erratics. Often, these rocks are scarred with scratches, gouges, and striations that bear witness to their tumultuous journey.

ARROWLEAF BALSAM ROOT

This pretty, sun-faced flower would be lovely anywhere, but it shines in its pairing with the rugged beauty of basalt.

A perennial, arrowleaf balsam root produces a brilliant yellow flower that reveals its membership in the sunflower family. It has arrow-shaped leaves up to a foot long, and the entire plant is covered with tiny hairs.

Balsam root is an edible plant but not much of a treat because of its bitter, pine-flavored sap. Native Americans dried and ground the flower's taproot into starchy flour, for use when other food was scarce. The sticky sap was also a topical antiseptic for minor wounds.

Balsam root graces the foot of high cliffs of Steamboat Rock, a giant, two hundred-foot-long block of basalt. The rock rises in terraces of columnar formations, forming plateaus that some believe look like the decks of a steamboat, hence the rock's name.

You can hike all the way to the table-flat top of Steamboat Rock, but it's no picnic; the trail rises eight hundred feet in one mile to reach the plateau. But consider the view, especially in spring, when the scablands freshen with gray-green sage lit by the yellow glow of balsam root.

Morning sun on arrowleaf balsam root in front of the basalt cliffs of Steamboat Rock State Park

Salmon have been called creatures of the forest, and while this may at first seem strange, the health of this fish depends absolutely on the health of the Northwest woods.

Trees, both living and dead, contribute much to the health of the salmon. Living, they shade the water and keep it cool, while tree roots hold stream banks so they do not erode and scour out in floods.

Fallen logs are also crucial to salmon health. Water plunges underneath or pours over large woody debris, varying the depth and velocity of the stream, which makes it attractive to a wider variety of salmon species. The debris also creates pools, used by fish to rest, hide, and find food, and helps retain gravel, which otherwise would be lost downstream. Gravel is used by salmon to create the nests, called redds, for their eggs.

Logs also provide overhead cover from predators, and they catch leaves, needles, twigs and other debris. This organic matter forms a base of the food chain, sustaining microbes, insects, and fish.

In main channels, fallen trees tend to ride the current, then stack along bends and gravel bars. They'll stay stuck there unless they become angled in the direction of the flow of the main channel and get swept further downstream.

The logjams built by rivers are amazingly strong and long lasting. I've hiked over logjams silver with age. Often these walls of wood are built of massive trees, and they aren't going anywhere for a long time. Even the wood that's submerged will last. Wood decomposes more slowly under water because of the lack of oxygen.

Salmon carcasses catch on logjams and rot, increasing the nutrients in the river, and becoming food for wildlife. Nitrogen from decomposing salmon carcasses also feeds the trees, completing the cycle of life.

Big Springs Creek waterfall with scattered, moss-covered logs, Gifford Pinchot National Forest

Twin Sisters Mountain, named for its ragged top, is well known to geologists, who regard it as one of the most unusual rock formations in the country.

The peaks, carved by glaciers, are a solid mass of dunite, a rare rock that consists almost entirely of the mineral olivine. This rock doesn't belong here. It is supposed to be stuffed in the mantle of the earth, not on display as a mountain. But there it is, weathered to a characteristic rusty brown, distinctive to the eye from afar.

Small grove of quaking aspen with red-osier dogwood in fall color, Wenatchee National Forest

QUAKING ASPEN

Aspens, radiant and yellow in the fall, are a gift of blazing gold. Their thin, smooth bark is nearly white, like bones, but it is the leaves that are this tree's star attraction. They shimmer and shiver in the slightest breeze.

Aspen are trees with good taste. They like the same choice real estate we do, tending to the banks of pristine rivers, forming swaths of gold that reflect in the sparkling water. Sometimes, as here, aspen grow in stands among colorful dogwood with their dried-berry crowns. They also glow against the dark gloom of conifers, and their leaves drift on the dark water in lazy, shining eddies.

Aspen are their most brilliant in the clear atmosphere of sunny Indian summer days. They blaze in the sunlight, and their leaves blow free and bright as tossed gold coins in the breeze.

Summer clouds building over Twin Sisters Mountain and the snow-covered peak of Mount Baker, Mount Baker–Snoqualmie National Forest

A soft duff of grasses, branch litter, and needles pads a ponderosa forest floor in eastern Washington. These dryland forests are different from the dense, soppy groves west of the Cascades.

Ponderosa pines form open, park-like expanses in the dryland forests because their roots crowd out other plants. The roots branch thickly from the trunk, taking what little moisture is available in dryland forests that bake like a furnace in summer and freeze solid in winter. The most drought and heat-tolerant of the pines, they grow in sunny groves east of the Cascades.

The cones of the ponderosa are sharp and pitchy, and so perfect they look like man-made decorations. The twigs will often carry a bit of soft green lichen, a delicate contrast to the gnarly, plated armor of the cones.

Ponderosas are venerable citizens, extremely slow growing and long-lived. Many have been around for centuries, and five-hundred-year-old trees abide.

My summer memories of these forests always include a hot, baking breeze, scented with the perfume of ponderosa. Lean in close to one on a summer day and the bark yields the strong, sweet smell of vanilla, while the needles and pitch add a hint of spice to the warm breeze. The light flickers through these open, graceful trees, while the wind sighs in the long, soft needles. There's breathing room in these forests, room to take a long stride without tripping over tangles of rotted logs. Or room to stretch out and take a nap in the shade of a grand old pine.

Ground detail of moss- and lichen-covered ponderosa branches with cones and needles, Lake Roosevelt National Recreation Area

Grove of ponderosa pines with dried grasses, Lake Roosevelt National Recreation Area

Fall-colored western larch on a granite
wall, Alpine Lakes Wilderness Area,
Wenatchee National Forest

I NEVER SAW A discontented tree. They grip the ground as though they liked it . . ."

—*John Muir,* John of the Mountains, *1938*

A SOOTHING POULTICE

Monkeyflower lights up any site it graces, growing in pink clumps wherever there is cold running water. A dancing stream is its favorite companion.

The cool juice of the crushed blossoms is a soothing poultice for scrapes and skin irritations; Native Americans used its crushed leaves and stems as a healing balm for sores. Monkeyflower was also cooked, to render its salty taste.

The flower's name comes from its face, which some liken to a smiling monkey. Its pink cheer is beautiful paired with soft disks of aster and the deep-velvet purple-blue of lupine.

A summer wildflower mix of monkeyflower, lupine, and aster along an intermittent stream, Mount Rainier National Park

The Channeled Scablands are the result of the most cataclysmic floods the world has ever seen, according to J. Harlen Bretz, a Washington geologist who studied the scablands in the 1920s. He determined nothing else could have formed this landscape but a flood of biblical dimensions.

Bretz called this event the Spokane Flood, and described it as a wall of water blasting across eastern Washington. For years, geologists scoffed at his theory. But in time, it was proven that glaciers on the move more than twelve thousand years ago dammed the Clark Fork River near the Idaho-Montana border. The lake that was formed, Glacial Lake Missoula, covered an area of about three thousand square miles and contained an estimated 480 cubic miles of water at its highest level, about the same volume as Lake Ontario. Its maximum depth was nearly two thousand feet, more than twice the depth of Lake Michigan. As the water rose, it eventually gained enough volume to float the ice dam, and break it, dumping massive amounts of water into eastern Washington.

Scientists, not known for hyperbole, describe what happened next as the most catastrophic flood of known geologic record. Swollen by the floodwaters, the Columbia River grew to contain ten times the flow of all the rivers of the world today. The Willamette Valley in Oregon was flooded as far south as present-day Eugene, and Portland would have been flooded under four hundred feet of water. Only the top ten floors of a forty-story building would have been high and dry, the floodwaters were so deep. Within a few years, glaciers impounded the Clark Fork River again to create another glacial lake and unleash yet another tirade of water.

Overlapping green hills descend to meet the waters of the Snake River, Asotin County

The Channeled Scablands are the result of these violent floods. Wherever the floodwater spilled, it swept away the soil, exposing the hard, black basalt beneath. In some places, the flood swept around both sides of a hill, leaving it standing as an island. Deep canyons called coulees were formed. They are the remaining dry basins of former waterfalls.

The Drumheller Channels is the most intricately eroded area of its size in the scablands. The ancient floodwaters carved a baroque vista of cliffs, canyons, and mesas that stretches on to the far distance. The Drumheller Channels was designated a National Natural Landmark in 1986.

Also sculpted by ancient floodwaters, the Snake River country in southeastern Washington is a heroic landscape of soaring open skies, the deeply carved canyon of towering basalt, and of course the mighty Snake River itself.

The flood that formed the Snake dates to fifteen thousand years ago. The

water charged through Red Rock Pass, south of Pocatello, Idaho, and, like the earlier floods, poured into the region in fantastic volume, scouring the canyon of the Snake River.

Today the Snake River is collared by four major hydroelectric dams in Washington State alone. In southeastern Washington, the Snake is not really a river at all, but a series of back-to-back reservoirs impounded by the big dams. The water is calm enough for the women's crew team at Washington State University to practice on the reservoir created by Lower Granite Dam.

Tame as the river may be, long stretches of the canyon still feel remote. From a boat on the Snake, you can watch the canyon roll by for miles and never see a house, a light, a person, or even a horse. It is an open landscape, carved by water and swept clean by the wind.

Late light on basalt cliffs and buttes above the grasslands of Drumheller Channels National Natural Landmark, Columbia National Wildlife Refuge

The Palouse country is a miracle of geology. Drive through these rolling wheat fields and it is like being at sea, watching waves of treeless green break against the sky.

The name of this region comes from the French word *pelouse,* meaning a beautifully kept playing field. This land *is* beautiful, whether fuzzed with the soft new green of spring planting, or bright with golden wheat waving in the summer sun. In winter the cut stubble pokes through drifted snow. The crystalline whiteness follows the drill lines of the plow, painting white, nested curves across the hillsides.

This landscape was formed during interglacial warm periods thirteen thousand to 1.8 million years ago. During these periods the climate was so dry that windstorms picked up and violently swirled glacial outwash sediments in the valleys and basins. Great dunes of silt called loess filled valleys and smothered nearly all but a few hilltops and basalt outcroppings. These deposits of wind-blown glacial dust and silt created the Palouse Formation.

The Palouse country covers an area eighty-five by one hundred miles, straddling the Idaho-Washington border. Its rich soil is a priceless inheritance that makes the Palouse one of the most fertile and productive agricultural regions in the world.

Morning light on white farm buildings nestled in the rolling hills of the Palouse country, Whitman County

CHAPTER 2

AIR

Clearing winter storm at sunset from Paradise overlooking
the Nisqually Valley and Cascade Range,
Mount Rainier National Park

M ENTION THE WORDS "Washington State" to anyone, and pretty soon, almost inevitably, the subject of weather will come next. Rain, specifically.

"Rains all the time!" people say about Washington, but it's not really true. Oh, sure, we'll get twelve feet of rain in one year. But only in the most water-logged spots on the so-called Wet Side, the west side of the Cascade Range. The mountains wring the clouds out on the windward side of the range, as storms barrel in from the Pacific.

Storms can brood and slash all day, then sweep clean at sunset. Lifting mists steam and smoke on the hills. The setting sun lights shifting, churning vapors, sheer and colorful as silk chiffon.

Fog sculpts a spectral landscape that eases in and out of view. Entire mountain ranges are painted out by the clouds.

The mountains create a rain shadow—a long stretch of country on the leeward side of the Cascades that is a baking, dry desert. Here the air is blindingly clear, and the sun stabs from skies white with heat.

All over the state, the air carries the scent of wild nature. Breathe deep the ferny green wet of the rain forest, the baking sage of the desert, and the clean, salt air of the sea.

The atmosphere of Washington is never just background. The air here is an active force of nature. It shapes the line of the land, defines the clarity of the light, and perfumes the breath of life.

Reflections of morning sun burning through fog on Lake Leo, Colville National Forest

There is a clarity to the summer skies in Washington that seems supernatural in its brightness. The sunsets in the San Juans reflect off still, jade green salt water, and the light burns to the very dome of the sky.

Perhaps it seems so clear, so colorful, because of the contrast to the silvery softness of the many gray, upholstered skies in winter. On a clear evening at sunset, every pine branch and leaf is silhouetted against a brilliant sky, like lead in stained glass. This wealth of light and cloud, this parade of weather, is one of the glories of living here.

Winter Skies

When clear skies do come in winter, they seem incredibly so, with all dust rinsed from the atmosphere, and the very air polished to crisp clarity. The refraction of pure light off snowy glaciers is brilliant. The air, scrubbed clean by the rain, seems newly minted, the essence of freshness. Clouds become impossible to imagine.

above
Rising winter moon over Twin Sisters Mountain with snow-covered forest, Mount Baker–Snoqualmie National Forest

right
Silhouetted fir and Pacific madrone trees against sunset sky from Turn Point on Stuart Island, San Juan Islands

View of Swift Creek canyon from
Kulshan Ridge, Mount Baker
Wilderness, Mount Baker–Snoqualmie
National Forest

Washington's famous clouds conspire well with its rolling hills to create sculptures of velvet green and cotton white. Cloud and mist pour like milk into the creases of the hills, and puddle there until the heat of the sun burns them off.

On some days, you can tell time here by the clouds. If the hills have not removed their wraps, the day is yet new.

COTTONWOOD PERFUME

Black cottonwoods are never so beautiful as when they are the perfect gold foil to lapis skies. But then, cottonwood can be beautiful in any weather. In storms it flips its leaves, showing their silvery white undersides.

The sap of cottonwood buds perfumes the spring air with a lush floral scent. I have always loved this fragrance, though I lived here for years before I could figure out where it was coming from. One spring evening I caught the distinctive perfume in the air and decided to follow it to its source. My nose led me down the road to a small tree by a stream, instead of to a drift of flowers or glorious flowering bush. Surprised, I buried my face in the branches, sniffing around to determine if the sapling could indeed be the source.

Sure enough. I followed my nose to tiny beads of clear sap, oozing from new leaves unfurling from their buds. I rubbed some thick and sticky sap on my wrists, so I could carry the elixir of spring with me. And I now know where to go back for more.

The many perfumes carried on the fresh Northwest air is one of the glories of living here. It smells of rain, it smells of wet ferns, new sap, fresh grass, spicy pines, and wet soil. Of tangy salt water, rank seaweed, and the deep duff of bigleaf maple leaves. Of sagebrush and the baking smell of sun-scorched grass.

There are a hundred different perfumes to enjoy every day, adrift on air fresh from the Pacific. They are different each hour of the day, and every one divine.

The golden leaves of black cottonwoods and blue sky reflected on the ice-textured surface of the Wenatchee River in late fall, Wenatchee National Forest

Eastern Washington's grasslands ripple under vast skies. This open landscape is a parade field for the march of weather.

In summer the heat fairly spoils for a fight, burning and searing day after day until rain clouds finally marshal on the horizon.

When the clouds come they can be deepest lavender, even nearly navy, signaling a gullywasher on the way that will green up the grasses again and coax wildflowers into bloom.

CASTLES IN THE AIR

The sagebrush country of eastern Washington is grand cloud-watching territory. Cumulus clouds stoked by summer heat build vast castles in the air.

On an overcast day, the sagebrush steppe is a palette of western colors, muted and sepia-toned. Purple-bellied clouds throw a silver light on gray-green sage and mauve-tinted basalt.

This rock, carved by ancient floodwaters, takes every shape: wedding cakes, prows of ships, pinnacles, spires, blocks, mesas, fat columns, organ pipes. The giant mesas are perfect pedestals for cloud sculptures rolled out by the winds.

left
Grasslands and sage-covered channel
under basalt cliffs, Drumheller
Channels National Natural Landmark

opposite page
Approaching storm clouds loom over
grasslands and distant channel lands,
Palouse Falls State Park

Moonrise with lenticular and cap clouds over Mount Shuksan in evening light, from Picture Lake, Mount Baker–Snoqualmie National Forest

Mount Shuksan and other peaks often wear so-called cap clouds just over their heads, snug as gossamer hats. Softly curved lenticular clouds also drift just overhead.

These clouds take shape when moisture-laden air, blown in from the Pacific coast, teams up with wavy wind patterns shaped by the mountain's hump.

Lenticular clouds are formed on the leeward side of the mountain, and cap clouds materialize near the summit as air is forced up the ridge. The air cools, condenses, and forms into a cloud above the peak. As it passes over the summit and rushes back down the slope, it warms, so the moisture evaporates. Condensation forms only over the peak, so the cloud forms and seems to remain stationary there.

Think of it as a plume of steam that remains visible at the top of a stack, even though the wind is really pushing the moisture along. The vapor replaces that which dissipates, so the cloud appears stationary.

Lenticular clouds are often a sign of a weather disturbance nearby; they usually mean a warm front is approaching. If followed by cirrus and stratus clouds, skiers, climbers, and others in the backcountry can generally take it as twenty-four to forty-eight hours notice of approaching rain or snow.

At sunset the beautiful, soft shapes of lenticular clouds look like space ships, hovering in a clear sky lit with soft alpenglow.

A ROBE OF CLOUDS

The face of Mount Rainier, called simply "The Mountain," changes with every passing cloud. It is astonishing that so large a mountain—the largest, in mass, in the Lower 48—could completely disappear in something as delicate as a cloud, but so it is.

Halolike clouds are another sign of oncoming rain, also forming when a warm front advances. The first clouds are very high wisps, called cirrus clouds. Their ice crystals or water droplets act as tiny prisms, bending and splitting sun and moonlight into their component colors. These halos, fairylike and magical, mean rain or snow is in the offing.

In evenings, after retiring behind a curtain of vapor all day, Rainier will sometimes poke out as if to say good night, while still keeping a robe of clouds drawn close about her shoulders.

Mount Rainier and Little Tahoma Peak encircled in a halo of clouds, Mount Rainier National Park

In Washington's West Side forests, moisture is constantly rising up from the ground, falling in sheets of rain, or cloaking every surface with mist. Ground-level clouds slip like ghosts through the treetops and pour down valleys, lacing the landscape with smoking, spectral fog. Even when it isn't raining, the mist will cruise in from the ocean and snuff out the sun.

These fog forests are swaddled in mist much of the year. Fog plays a huge role in their ecology.

Fog elevates humidity in the tree canopy, making it a less stressful environment, which is beneficial to tree health. Mosses, lichens, and ferns are able to grow well, because there is plenty of moisture for them to absorb through their foliage.

Fog also changes the nature of light in the forest. On clear, sunny days, light is direct; the canopy gets most of the sun, and the forest floor remains dim. But in fog, the light is diffused, so much more light gets to the middle and the bottom of the canopy. Light also enters the forest from many more angles. The fog acts as millions of tiny prisms, refracting and diffusing the light so it is present not only at the top of the canopy, but at middle and lower levels too. This soft light is perfect for lush plant growth. Teamed with abundant moisture, it is a recipe for the rankly thick growth found in coastal fog forests.

Fog in the air adds greatly to the amount of moisture that winds up on the ground. Fog condenses on billions of conifer needles, which comb it from the air in brilliant drops. The moisture falls to the earth in a fine, persistent drip.

Rainmaking by trees, or fog drip as the scientists call it, is no small matter. In parts of the Hoh Rainforest, researchers say fog condensation annually adds about thirty inches of moisture. That's almost as much rainfall as downtown Seattle sees in a year. Fog drip can add as much as 30 percent of the annual precipitation rate soaked up by the forest.

Fog wrapping itself around an evergreen forest and small cascading stream, Mount Rainier National Park

Western hemlock, Washington's state tree, wears moss well. A denizen of the deep gloom, hemlock will sprout and thrive in the mist and dim light of the rain forest floor, where other tree seedlings languish.

Hemlock likes nothing better than dense shade and eight or nine months of rain, fog, mist, and drip followed by a few months of coolness we call summer.

It is a dark, nearly black, green tree and swaths the land in a dark cloak hung with draperies of moss. Western hemlock's tiny, closely set needles throw the blackest shade, an astonishing darkness. A dense canopy of western hemlock clotted with moss will produce twilight at noon.

The gloom and wet of a hemlock grove is home to all the shade-loving species and creatures. Slugs, moss, ferns, and mushrooms all love the dim atmosphere of a hemlock forest. The shade shuts out the sun that would dry the dampness—and that's just perfect for growing even more hemlock seedlings, to throw thicker, wetter gloom.

Big Spring Creek flowing through moss-draped hemlock forest, Gifford Pinchot National Forest

Detail of frosted hemlock branches,
Mount Baker–Snoqualmie National
Forest

A trip through the high country in winter is a trip through an evergreen wonderland, with every detail of the black green hemlock highlighted with brilliant white.

All the moisture so typical of western Washington combined with the altitude of the high country makes the cold an artist.

Moist air freezes into millions of tiny ice crystals that coat every surface in sparkling hoarfrost. Meteorologists have a term for this: They call the transformation of water vapor directly into ice crystals "deposition." You could also call it simply beautiful.

There is rapture on the lonely shore,
There is society, where none intrudes,
By the deep sea, and music in its roar:
I love not man the less, but Nature
    more.
        —Lord Byron, *Childe Harold's Pilgrimage*

Sunset afterglow at Beach 4, Olympic National Park

CHAPTER 3

FIRE

Volcanic basalt stones in a golden field, Klickitat Wildlife Area,
Klickitat County

F IRE HAS SHAPED Washington's landscape, and will shape it again, in ways beyond our power to control or even imagine.

It takes artistic license, blazing in prisms of ice that cling to hoarfroasted branches.

It transforms water into fire through sunlight cast back from mirror-bright pools, ripples, and waves.

It burns bright in wildflowers that paint alpine meadows. Trees in fall color blaze against the black green of fir and hemlock forests.

The serrated silhouettes of the Cascade and Olympic Ranges saw at fiery sunset skies.

Fire also works the land with a heavier hand.

Millions of years ago, fire shaped much of eastern and central Washington, when massive seas of molten lava flooded the land, then cooled to form sculptures of basalt. This landscape is so rugged that when pictures of Mars were first beamed back to Earth, scientists were quick to find their look-alike in Washington's Channeled Scablands.

Fire is still a force to be reckoned with today.

Blazes ignited by lightning govern the health of the forests, killing bugs that infest trees and clearing dead and down organic matter that could stoke infernos nature did not intend.

In the future, Washington's volcanoes, part of the Pacific Ring of Fire, may wreak destruction only glimpsed with the eruption of Mount St. Helens in 1980.

The fiery forces of nature reminds us that nature always bats last.

Fall colors of a vine maple on a hillside in a spruce and hemlock forest, Mount Rainier National Park

The fire of the sun's reflection camouflages the cool, green haven of these aquatic grasses. Fiery sunlight, glinting off blades of grass, disguises this limpid, quiet pool. The brilliant light plays tricks with the eye, and with the landscape itself. What is water looks like fire. What is wet and cool appears ablaze with light.

These freshwater pools, alive with aquatic grasses, are cool sanctuaries below their brilliant surface. They provide essential food and habitat for waterfowl and fish. Aquatic grasses are also the nursery for tiny invertebrate life forms that build a base of the freshwater food chain.

WESTERN LARCH

Does larch burn hotter in the fireplace or in its autumnal blaze? It is hard to say.

Western larch, *Larix occidentalis*, also called western tamarack, is a star of the Northwest woods in the fall. It is the only coniferous tree in the Northwest to turn color in autumn and lose its needles. And what a color it turns.

Larch form towering torches that burn an incandescent yellow, vivid against the black green of pine, hemlock, and fir. Their autumnal quick-change artistry makes this tree a surprise. It turns up vivid yellow on a hillside you thought was just . . . green.

Western larches in brilliant autumn gold on the slopes of the Kettle Mountains at Sherman Pass, Colville National Forest

Silver patterned reflections of aquatic grasses on the surface of Picture Lake at Heather Meadows, Mount Baker–Snoqualmie National Forest

RAIN SHADOWS

Evening light on rocky cliffs of Turn Point above the Haro Strait, Stuart Island, San Juan Islands

Many of the San Juan Islands bake under the searing heat of the summer sun, while rain forests on the nearby Olympic Peninsula will easily see twelve feet of rain annually. The San Juans are located within the Olympic rain shadow, and receive only fifteen to twenty-nine inches of annual rainfall. Most of the moisture is wrung out of the clouds as they climb the western side of the range; land on the east side is dry. The rain shadow also causes a perpetual break in the cloud cover—what pilots call "the blue hole"—over Sequim, a city on the Olympic Peninsula so dry cacti grow in the torched grass.

The Nooksack

This fast, cold river looks black as it cuts through the fire-bright sunlit ice and snow. Come closer and it shows its true green colors, and the darker grays, black, and browns of the cobbles and gravel of the river bottom.

Glaciers carved the river valley and quarried much of this rock.

The headwaters of the Nooksack are in the heart of the North Cascades National Park. The river pulses with glacial meltwater from the icy mantle of Mount Baker. This Cascade Range volcano, capable of so much fiery destruction, feeds clean, cold water from its shoulders of ice to the Nooksack. It courses through the lowland forests, a river born of fire and ice.

Winter morning sun on frosted branches along the snow-covered banks of the North Fork of the Nooksack River, Mount Baker–Snoqualmie National Forest

Sea stacks form a gap-toothed coastline that splits the light of the setting sun into chunks and reflects its fiery color off the wet shine of sea-sprayed rock faces.

I love the mystery of sea stacks. Their shapes are sometimes graceful, sometimes gnarled and tortured. Some look exactly like seals, turning to look over their shoulders. Others look like the sail of a ship. They give the Northwest coast a wild, primitive look that changes with every shifting cloak of mist or angle of sunlight.

Sunset silhouetting sea stacks on Rialto Beach, Olympic National Park

above
Pastel colors of dried grasses in an open
meadow, Lake Roosevelt National
Recreational Area

Aridity, more than anything else, gives the western landscape its character. It is aridity that gives the air its special dry clarity; aridity that puts brilliance in the light and polishes and enlarges the stars; aridity that leads the grasses to evolve as bunches rather than turf. . . ."

—*Wallace Stegner,* Where the Bluebird Sings to the Lemonade Springs, *1992*

Contrasts

opposite page
Kangaroo Ridge in evening light above
the golden grasses of Washington
Meadows at Washington Pass,
Okanogan National Forest

In the high country, the sun burns bright on the ridges above even as you walk in shadow. These contrasts in light and dark, warmth and cold are part of the magic of hiking in the high country.

When pitching camp, I often try to figure out where the sun will first light the ground. Which is worse: to shiver waiting for the morning sun, or shiver watching it shine on the opposite hill?

The dampness of morning shade never seems so chill as when the ridge just above burns with warm golden light.

Vine maple along the Stillaguamish
River, Mount Baker–Snoqualmie
National Forest

BURNING LEAVES

The vine maple is a loner, seldom growing in groups. It is short lived: Its time on the planet is not much longer than ours. And it is a spindly thing.

But what it lacks in stature it makes up for in fall color. The brilliant foliage of vine maple burns like embers in a dark wood. Its brilliant leaves glow on the forest floor and float like sparks on dark water.

Vine maple leaves in autumn, Mount Baker–Snoqualmie National Forest

FIREWEED

Fireweed is a pioneer plant, a harbinger of new life. It is usually among the first plants to colonize burned-over land, hence its name. A member of the evening primrose family, it also establishes easily in disturbed soils, such as roadsides and fields. But it is most common in old fire burns and logged-over areas. Fireweed helps stabilize the soil and begin a new cycle of succession.

Fireweed will stand quite tall at two to even nine feet in a site it likes. The individual flower stalks are crowded with purple-pink to rose-lilac blooms that flower progressively upward. The color advances like a slow-burning fire.

The leaves are dark green, narrow and lancelike and can be as long as eight inches. Its long slender seedpods produce hundreds of seeds borne on white, fluffy tufts that carry the seed on the breeze.

Fireweed is one of the most common wildflowers in the Pacific Northwest. It blooms all summer long, lighting up even desolate clear-cuts with the delicate, waving wands of its bright purple flowers.

I love to walk old logging roads with my dog Molly in the summer, with fireweed blossoms waving at us as we pass, like blessings.

FRIENDLY FIRE

Once suppressed by forest managers, fire is now understood to be a key element of forest health. Fire kills bugs and clears deadwood from the forest floor, which, if allowed to accumulate, fuels disastrous wildfires. The heat of a forest fire is also the only key that will unlock the seed casings of some pine cones.

Fire does not bring death to a forest as much as it brings new life, a beginning of a new cycle of succession. In a healthy forest, fire will not kill all the trees. Some will be spared by shifts of the wind, a lucky roll of the topography, or by bark plated thick as armor. Larch often survives fire because of its thick bark with many overlapping plates.

In their brilliant yellow fall foliage, these larch look like flames in the remains of a charred wood.

Surviving western larch in fall color on a hillside of the White Mountain Burn, Colville National Forest

Fireweed and pearly everlasting, Mount Baker–Snoqualmie National Forest

The golden fall foliage of bracken fern will deepen as autumn settles into winter.

While other ferns stay evergreen throughout the winter, bracken fern dies back to its roots, leaving heaps of bronze and purple-tinged sculpture.

Come spring the ferns will send up tall stems, topped with fuzzy, claw-shaped new growth that lengthens and spreads to lovely, branching foliage. Fully grown, bracken fern will stand hip-high and taller.

The perennial roots run horizontally for long distances underground, and are as thick as a man's middle finger. The roots are black on the outside and have a white, glutinous material at their heart, shot through with tough, longitudinal fibers.

The plants form dense thickets that provide good cover for birds. Bracken fern was also an important food for Native Americans.

Virtually all coastal tribes used the rhizomes for food, usually digging them in the late fall or winter. The rhizomes would be coiled and allowed to dry. Later they would be roasted in an open fire until the outer skin could be peeled off. Then the inner parts were pounded with a stick. After removing the tough central fibers, the whitish starchy inside was eaten, usually with fish eggs or seal oil.

Some tribes even made a type of bread from bracken fern by pounding the roasted roots into flour, mixing it with water, and forming the dough into flat cakes, which were roasted.

Fall color of bracken ferns and vine
maple, Alpine Lakes Wilderness Area,
Wenatchee National Forest

Umatilla Rock towering above a
hillside of sage and dried grasses, Sun
Lakes State Park

The golden dry cheat grass that has insinuated itself in the sagebrush steppes is an enemy of this fragile habitat.

Cheat grass is an invasive plant that crowds out native bunch grass. It is very difficult to eradicate. Cheat grass has many seeds and a competitive advantage over bunch grass because it can germinate in lower temperatures.

It forms a solid cover, unlike bunch grasses, which grow in clumps to minimize surface moisture loss. These pavings of solid cheat grass increase the danger of wildfire.

Fire will stall out in bunch grass, because it has no fuel between clumps. But in thick masses of cheat grass, the fire will leap across acres. When lightning strikes, it's not unusual for ten thousand acres stoked with tinder-dry cheat grass to burn at a time.

These fires are hotter, because they are bigger. They will burn the native sagebrush to a pile of white ash. Once destroyed by fire, sagebrush cannot grow back from the root. It must germinate from seed, and viable seed can be far away when large areas of sagebrush country have been sterilized by fire. Re-vegetation is slow and difficult.

A KAYAK AND THE SAN JUANS

Fiery sunsets silhouette the soft shapes of the seascape of the San Juan Islands.

This archipelago is comprised of 768 rocks, reefs, and islands at low tide. When the tide rushes back in, many islands drown. Only 475 remain above water.

Much of this saltwater-rinsed island paradise is quite wild. Only 175 of the San Juans have names, and only about 50 are populated. The state ferry system serves a few of the islands, but many can only be reached by private boat, seaplane, or kayak. I like that part.

The kayaking is delightful here. I once stuffed my tiny boat with everything I needed for an overnight trip and paddled through clear, green salt water with the sound of porpoise puffing in my ear.

The kelp beds sighed on the tide and the quiet was absolute.

It was a good long paddle to James Island, a marine state park. When I got there I made a huge steaming vat of macaroni and cheese over my camp stove, hung my wet clothes in a tree, and fell deeply asleep in a goose-down sleeping bag to the sound of the tide sorting beach stones.

In the morning an otter slipped over the beach where I drank my coffee, and bald eagles called to each other overhead. Magic.

Sunset afterglow reflecting on Rosario Strait, from Deception Pass State Park, Whidbey Island, San Juan Islands

Giant red paintbrush, a wildflower common in the meadows at Mount Rainier, blazes away like a hot poker in the dampest mist.

Paintbrush, a member of the snapdragon family, grows to a height of two feet and flowers with scarlet-tipped bracts from April through July. It loves meadows and prairies, and its colorful blooms look like fat brushes dipped in bright paint—hence their name.

Paintbrush is part of a giant family of plants with at least two hundred species that are partially or wholly parasitic. They take their nourishment from other plants and so are no choice for the home garden.

They have been used by Native Americans for everything from rheumatism to secret love charms.

Its companion, the creamy white valerian, has a distinctive odor about its roots, which some liken to dirty gym socks or, to be kinder about it, a strong, earthy scent.

Indian tribes of the Northwest cooked and ate the leaves and roots of valerian, but the plant is not very palatable; the flavor is like its odor.

But then, valerian is valued not for food, but for its sedative qualities. Valerian is perhaps the best-known herbal sedative in the world. It has been used for hundreds of years as a remedy for stress, muscle tension, insomnia, and anxiety. Modern folks who fear air travel have been known to take a bit along for the ride.

Wild animals also eat valerian to take the edge off their day, some botanists believe.

A mix of summer wildflowers including giant red paintbrush, valerian, lousewort, and asters on Mazama Ridge near the town of Paradise, Mount Rainier National Park

Yellow lichen coloring columnar basalt
cliffs of Steamboat Rock, Steamboat
Rock State Park

Basalt is the unmistakable, rugged resident artist of eastern Washington.

It is a black rock, but you'd never know that by looking at it, because basalt is always stained rusty brown by the iron oxide in the stone. The black color appears only on freshly broken surfaces.

Basalt formations are the result of lava flows that blanketed eastern and central Washington. Most of the lava erupted during the Miocene Epoch, between about 17 million and 6 million years ago. The lava erupted from long, wide fissures in the earth and flowed onto the hilly terrain of older rocks. The early flows filled the valleys. More flows followed and covered most of the high hills. The lava was so fluid that some streamed all the way to the Pacific Ocean. Layers of lava piled up, eventually forming a solid sea of basalt, in places becoming more than two miles thick. The sheer volume of lava was astounding. Some individual flows thicker than seventy-five feet covered more than one hundred miles.

The basalt formed a myriad of shapes as the molten lava cooled. Thin lava flows broke into single rows of columns. The lava cooled first at the top, then at the bottom, cracking into vertical polygons, most with five or six sides.

The most frequently seen formation comes from thicker flows, which separated into two rows of columns, with a band of irregular, broken basalt in between. The rows of columns form ledges that stack hundreds of feet high, like a wedding cake.

The individual columns can range quite a bit in size, even throughout a single formation. Some columns are as big around as a barrel. Others are squat pipes, and still other flows formed countless small, tight blocks and cells. Where basalt flowed into water, it cooled rapidly, forming pillows.

Today, formations of the cooled lava dominate the landscape of central and eastern Washington, as well as parts of Idaho and Oregon. The dense, crystalline lava covers more than one hundred thousand square miles.

I once lived in a small place with a big view, with my desk given the place of honor: a picture window framing an unobstructed view of volcanic Mount Rainier.

I watched this mountain every day, keeping track of its many moods, its endlessly varied wardrobe of cloud cover, and the soft or brilliant light on its glaciated sides. In the evening, the setting sun would sometimes throw alpenglow over the mountain from foothills to summit. The mountain looked lit from within, with its glaciers shimmering in soft pink light.

Mount Rainier is 14,410 feet high and the largest and most dangerous volcano in the country. It rattles and shakes with more than one hundred earthquakes annually. It is expected to erupt again one day, sending catastrophic mudslides over much of the Puget Sound region.

But it's still a beautiful neighbor.

Volcanoes and Glaciers

The fire and ice of glaciers brilliant with alpenglow is a treasure of the North Cascades.

Mount Baker, 10,775 feet high, watches over the northern end of the Cascade Range. Its striking cone clad in sparkling white glaciers—about twenty of them—dominates the horizon. On a very clear day the perfect cone of Baker can be seen from Vashon Island, southwest of Seattle. The volcano floats dreamlike above Puget Sound, shimmering white and enormous even from a distance of seventy-five miles.

Baker constantly emits small quantities of steam, often forming a small cloud over its peak. In 1975, Baker sparked a false alarm when the volcano began to blow off a plume of steam visible for miles. Small quantities of ash also darkened the plume, and for a while the volcano produced more than a ton of sulfurous gases per hour.

The volcano seemed to be awakening, but it was a mirage. The steam was not as hot as that generated during an eruption, and the ash was old material, not new. It was just a sigh, the mountain blowing off surface water that had soaked into its face and hit hot rocks in its interior.

The beautiful mantle of ice that drapes Baker and the other Cascade volcanoes is exactly what makes them so dangerous. Glacier-covered summits increase the hazards of an eruption because the ice could melt and form a volcanic mudflow called a lahar.

During an eruption, snow and ice are transformed to water and steam,

Mount Rainier from an alpine meadow with fallen trees, beargrass, and pink mountain heather, Mount Rainier National Park

which mixes with hot ash and rock debris to make a slurry. Gravity takes over, and the resulting lahar can tear down the mountain at speeds of fifty miles an hour, destroying everything in its path.

Sudden release of intense hot gasses is another danger of volcanic eruptions. The heat can be so intense, the fiery breath of the volcano incinerates every living thing on its flanks.

Mount Baker glaciers in evening light over summer meadow of valerian, Mount Baker Wilderness, Mount Baker–Snoqualmie National Forest

This vast crater is testimony to Mount St. Helens' violent eruption on May 18, 1980. Once the smallest and loveliest of the Cascade volcanoes, St. Helens blew a hole in her north side that day and shattered her symmetrical shape.

Signs of the eruption began in March 1980, as the volcano began to vent clouds of steam. This, in itself, was not a sure sign that an eruption was near. Volcanoes will steam when surface water comes in contact with hot interior rocks.

But when a swarm of earthquakes shook the mountain, geologists took notice.

The clouds of steam also became steadily darker and hotter. That suggested molten rock, or magma, might be rising in the volcano. Seismographic readings showed tremors deep inside the volcano, which also suggested magma on the move.

April went by, and the clouds of steam grew darker still. Meanwhile a bulge began to grow on the volcano's north side. Geologists were sure it was formed by rising magma, but they still could not be sure whether the volcano would erupt.

As the bulge grew, so did the likelihood of a landslide.

On the morning of May 18, steam began rising from the bulge, and the snow covering it began to melt rapidly. The north side of the mountain started to slip while steam, black with ash, shot out at the head of the landslide. The entire north side of the volcano exploded, with a blast so violent it flattened most of the surrounding forest.

The eruption released energy equivalent to twenty-one thousand atomic bombs like the one that destroyed Hiroshima, geologists say. The north face of St. Helens raged down the mountain at about two hundred miles an hour, stuffing the North Fork of the Toutle River. The mudflow raced all the way to the Columbia River, forty-five miles away, where it piled up deeply enough to clog navigation channels.

A massive cloud of ash billowed into the air and blew eastward, darkening the sky and falling like snow all day and through the night over a wide swath of eastern Washington, northern Idaho, and western Montana.

The cone of St. Helens, once the most perfect in the Cascade Range and 9,677 feet high, stood shattered and 1,300 feet lower after the eruption.

Today the volcano is magnificent in a new way, as a living monument to the stupendous forces of nature.

Mount St. Helens's steaming lava dome, crater, and lava flows from the Johnston Ridge Observatory, Mount St. Helens National Volcanic Monument

CHAPTER 4

WATER

Silhouetted sea stacks of Ruby Beach at sunset reflected
in the still water of Cedar Creek, Olympic
National Park

WASHINGTON'S RIVERS WIND in silver ribbons that tie the state together from the high country to the low, all the way to the sea.

Clean, cold water is the key to abundant and healthy ecosystems in all of these habitats. The glaciers of the high country and abundant rain and snow feed icy cold streams that join to form the state's many rivers, with names as beautiful as their waters: Skykomish, Stillaguamish, Skagit, Skokomish, Columbia, Snake, Yakima, Kettle, Wenatchee, and Little Spokane, to name only a few.

Where the rivers meet the sea, estuaries provide a unique habitat of salt and fresh water crucial to a vast variety of fish, sea creatures, and birds.

The Pacific pounds at a rugged shore. Sea stacks stud the nearshore water, forming a toothy coastline. These ancient rock formations were used by eighteenth-century explorers as navigation tools. Their distinctive shapes can be seen for miles.

Much of the coast is still completely wild, and looks as it always has.

Elsewhere, use and abuse of the land and water is the greatest challenge to the continued viability of the ecosystems all creatures, including ourselves, depend on.

By now, nearly every major river in the state is home to a species of fish listed for protection under the Endangered Species Act.

The first hundred years of Washington's statehood were about taming the essential elements of nature to our use. The next will be about balance, restoration, and preservation of Washington's great gift: water.

Winter sun backlighting the snow-covered trees along the North Fork of the Nooksack River, Mount Baker–Snoqualmie National Forest

Waterfalls are a signature of Washington wildlands. These chutes of water spill in bridal veils of icy wet down hundreds of canyons, mountainsides, and cliffs. The music of this tumbling water will be heard on almost any hike in western Washington, where melting glaciers, abundant rainfall, basalt cliffs, cirques, and canyon walls conspire to compose the crashing wet music of waterfalls.

But western Washington does not hold a monopoly on waterfalls. People just think it does.

A brilliant white plume of fresh water is the last thing a hiker expects in this desert scabland, and Palouse Falls indeed comes as a surprise in the sun-baked sagebrush hills of eastern Washington. But there it is, 190 feet of grandeur, crashing into a deep, dark-green pool that swallows it whole, greedily. From this unlikely pool at the center of a rock-rimmed amphitheater, the water gathers itself and rushes on as the Palouse River, shooting through a narrow channel it has carved through one hundred-foot-thick lava flows of columnar basalt.

Overall, there are more than seven hundred waterfalls mapped in the four northwestern states.

The Cascade Range takes its name from falling water, and many visitors take the music of Washington waterfalls with them when they go.

Gorge Creek Falls above Gorge Lake and the Upper Skagit River, Ross Lake National Recreation Area

View of Palouse Falls through a grass-covered basalt crevice, Palouse Falls State Park

Winter creeps in quietly in the high country, gradually taking hold of the land.

The first snows of winter ice down the glowing colors of fall before autumn has even left the high country. Snow ushers in the silent season, when the only sound deep in the woods is the rush of a stream or thunk of snow sliding off a branch into eiderdown drifts. This first dusting will be gone in hours, and the fall colors will burn all the brighter, stoked by the colder night temperatures. But the snow has regained its ground. Soon, it will be back in force, and these colors will be long gone, given up to a perfect whiteness.

The crystal brilliance of ice also moves in slowly as the days shorten and turn colder. Ice is the artisan of winter, sculpting and glazing the ordinary into the fantastic. Skipping a rock on an early ice-up brings a high-pitched reverberation you won't hear in deep winter, when the ice thickens. The flow of cold water under the ice, breaking through in dark sluicing pools is a beautiful thing to see, a last glimpse of free-flowing water before ice locks it up tight.

In the high country, snow piles on ice, shouldering across the channel until only pockets of dark, moving water can still be heard singing in the deep winter quiet. Everything has changed—slowly, gradually, but inexorably.

Growing ice patterns encircling rocks at the edge of the North Fork of the Nooksack River, Mount Baker–Snoqualmie National Forest

Fresh snow on fall-colored hillside and
firs at Heather Meadows, Mount Baker
National Recreation Area, Mount
Baker–Snoqualmie National Forest

View of Mount Shuksan and
contoured rain patterns in snow near
Austin Pass, Mount Baker–Snoqualmie
National Forest

Great, glorious soakings of precipitation shape the landscape of the North Cascades, giving rise to the glaciers that mantle the mountains and the avalanches that rumble down the peaks.

These mountains are only moderately high, yet they are covered with ice. In fact, the glaciation is more extensive in the North Cascades than on higher mountains at similar latitude, because the North Cascades are closer to the Pacific Ocean, a massive source of moisture. Fog, rain, mist, and snow dump a total of about 110 inches of precipitation a year on average on the western side of the range. It's not unusual for more than thirty feet of snow to fall in a single winter.

Rain or snow in late spring produces delicate patterns, pummeled into the snow by heavy drops. Rain also drips from branches in emphatic splats that carve the snowy surface.

In exceptional years, snowfall and snowpack throughout the Cascade Range can reach fantastic depths. During the 1971–72 snow season, the Paradise Ranger Station at 5,500 feet of elevation on the west side of Mount Rainier recorded snowfall of 1,122 inches.

Not surprisingly with such exceptional amounts of snow, avalanches are common in the Cascades. Sometimes after such an avalanche comes to rest at the base of a mountain, a snow cave develops.

Snow caves are formed when meltwater runs beneath the snow, forming a hole in the drift. These caves are often all that remains of snow avalanche deposits that accumulate to deep depths.

Eventually, moving water and drafts of warm air rushing through the cave will enlarge it, until the roof becomes so thin it collapses.

The caves invite trespass. But despite their appeal, snow caves are places to be watched from afar instead of explored within—they are dangerous places. Roofs fall in, and rocks, cascading down the mountains, crash through their snowy architecture.

Storm King and Goode Mountain with Goode Glacier from North Fork Meadows along the North Fork of Bridge Creek, North Cascades National Park

View of ice cave and hillside meadow framed by bigleaf maple and black cottonwood trees in the Cascade River canyon, North Cascades National Park

Rushing glacial streams lace the high country of the Cascade Range, whose highest peaks are mantled with glaciers year round. Meltwater from the Cascade glaciers gathers into streams that cut channels down the mountainsides. The daily cycle of melting makes stream crossings dangerous in the afternoon, during peak melting of ice and snow.

The water is full of minerals from glacial flour—the fine rock powder milled by tons of grinding ice. It makes the meltwater a palette of colors, from deep green, to bright blue, brilliant aqua, electric teal, or milky white. Other, non-glacial meltwater streams run with a clear purity that dances with light.

Glacial streams are crucial to wildlife, including salmon. The juvenile salmon, called smolts, depend on the cold runoff of ice and snow to flush them to the sea in the spring.

These streams are a vital part of the hydrologic cycle. Water evaporates from the ocean, then falls to the earth as rain or snow. The water is stored in glaciers and snowpack, or runs off in glacial meltwater and rainfall. The runoff and melt-water gather in mountain streams that find their way to rivers. They run to the sea, and the cycle begins anew.

Rivers and streams are the vital link between the high country and the low, between the mountains and the sea. Sever or block any of these connections, and it matters. The sound of clean, free-flowing water is the sound of a healthy eco-system.

Meltwater from Washington's wildlands also provides much of the water cities, farms, and hydroelectric plants need. We depend as much on the hydro-logic cycle as the wild creatures, including salmon, that evolved with it.

The North Fork of glacier-fed Bridge Creek, North Cascades National Park

Water is the sculptor and percussionist of Washington's beaches.

The outgoing tides grasp and claw at the rock cover of the beach, tumbling the cobbles smooth. From fist-sized rocks to gleaming black-and-gray pebbles, these stones are the timpani of the surf, drummed and rattled around by pounding waves.

Stretches of Beach 4, part of the coastal wonderland of Olympic National Park, are littered with the clunky cobblestones. The beach is steep, encouraging a heavy, dumping surf that breaks close to shore. A thick bed of stones, pebbles, and larger cobbles provide bright, percussive notes to accompany the roar of waves.

Giant stumps and logs from old-growth trees also reverberate with the booming tide. The massive size of old-growth logs found on Pacific beaches is testament to the power of the ocean. These huge logs are tossed like matchsticks in the powerful surf. They are sculptures without edges, tumbled smooth by the tide.

Washington's rugged coast is home to the most dramatic heaps of polished driftwood anywhere. When soaked through with winter rainstorms and crashing storm tides, driftwood feels thick and soft as leather. As the summer sun dries the wood, it turns a satiny silver-gray.

The origin of these boneyards of the Pacific is an invitation to wonder. Some of the logs are refugees from log booms. Others were flushed to the sea by upland floods. Some of them washed ashore from miles away and will stay a decade or more on the same beach. Then they disappear in a seething storm.

Driftwood piles are the raw material of dreams and the supply store for the beach forts and hideaways that are the work of every coastal kid. These silver heaps can tower shoulder high and invite afternoons of scrambling, climbing, and collecting. Driftwood also decorates the homes of many lifelong residents of the Washington coast. And nothing compares to the perfume of a beach fire of driftwood, sending sparks into the gloaming as surf purls the sand.

Water-worn rocks and pockets exposed at low tide on Beach 4, Olympic National Park

Weathered driftwood scattered among
the rocks of Ruby Beach, Olympic
National Park

In the dim, damp drip of the Quinault River valley, deep in the rain forest of Olympic National Park, it's always twilight. Dense curtains of moss drape the watery thin light that strains through sheets of rain.

The Quinault is one of four rain forest valleys in the park. About ten to fifteen feet of rain fall in the Quinault Rainforest—called the Quinault Rain Barrel by the locals—every year. Much of this rain falls in drizzle and soft showers that gently glaze the forest. But it also thunders, roars, and drips in clattering splats, only to trail off in a mist so fine the forest becomes a vast, steamy terrarium.

The climate is mild, so the lush growth stoked by all that moisture never perishes under a deep freeze. It just gets . . . thicker.

REFUGE

The Nisqually National Wildlife Refuge protects the fragile estuary formed where the Nisqually River empties into Puget Sound. The lower watershed was sculpted about fifteen thousand years ago by the carving and grinding action of the Vashon Ice Sheet, which covered much of southern Puget Sound. As the glacier advanced and retreated it created coarse, gravely soils and flattened the landscape.

Today the Nisqually River and two neighboring creeks form one of the largest, most important estuarine habitats left in Washington. While most major estuaries have been filled, dredged, or developed, the federal government protected a wide variety of fish and wildlife habitats with the creation of the Nisqually River National Wildlife Refuge in 1974.

The refuge is an important island of conservation amid the heavy development of the populous Puget Sound region. It is a haven for migratory birds, who stop, feed, and rest here before continuing their journey. Some migratory birds, such as western sandpipers and other shorebirds, rest and feed on estuarine mud flats and marshes. Ducks, geese, and herons thrive in the freshwater ponds and wetlands. Songbirds, including goldfinches, warblers, and tree swallows, flourish in the upland forests. Non-migratory birds, such as woodpeckers, hawks, bald eagles, and osprey, also call the refuge home. This special place is a refuge not only for wildlife, but also for people craving quiet, open sky, and the whisper of bird wings beating in soft twilight.

Twilight colors reflect on the Nisqually delta at McAllister Creek, Nisqually National Wildlife Refuge

Moss-covered bigleaf maple and
redwood sorrel ground cover, Quinault
River valley, Olympic National Park

The tranquillity of hundreds of coves in the San Juan Islands is a treasure that year-round residents of the islands are determined to protect.

In 1998 San Juan Islanders made national news by implementing the first ban on personal watercraft in the country. It was a grassroots victory that began with the determination of one couple intent on keeping Jet Skiers' noisy machines from turning the bay outside the couple's window into a Disneyland ride gone amuck. Far better, they felt, to hear the surfing and spouting of orcas and porpoise.

It took three years of lawsuits and appeals to make the ban stick, but islanders remained determined to protect these quiet coves as much as possible, despite the pressures of tourism and development. The ban went into effect in October 1998.

Evening light on sandstone headlands
of Sucia Island, San Juan Islands

Fern Cove, on Vashon Island, is home to thirteen and one-half acres of exceptional habitat diversity, including upland forests, riparian areas, a saltwater marsh, cobbled beaches, a fan delta with eelgrass beds, and a saltwater estuary.

The forest is packed with ninety- to one-hundred-year-old second-growth Douglas fir, western hemlock, and western red cedar that tower above the cold, green salt water.

This pretty place is home to soaring bald eagles, the clatter of kingfishers, and the primordial squawk of great blue herons. Black brant, snow geese, and common loons all use the estuary for their kitchen, and the water is alive with harbor seals and river otters, sea-run cutthroat trout, and coho salmon.

Islanders rallied when landowners announced plans to sell Fern Cove for development. A nonprofit citizens' group called the Friends of Fern Cove formed to work with local and state government to purchase the property for preservation. Because of their efforts, the music of tumbling streams and blowing trees will not stop, and the eagles, kingfishers, and herons will keep coming here. Fern Cove's unique values for wildlife habitat and human reflection are preserved forever.

LEAF LITTER

Leaf litter plays a vital role in stream health.

The clear-rushing streams that crisscross Washington forests are stocked with tiny insects and invertebrates needed by fish, including salmon. Decomposing leaves provide some of the food for these tiny creatures, creating an essential link in the food chain.

Scientists now understand the importance of woody debris and organic material, including leaf litter, to salmon. Biologists and state fish managers used to clear streams of logs and other organic debris, believing it blocked fish passage. Little by little streams were robbed of the organic material that builds a base of the food chain.

Today, logs are deliberately felled into streams, or placed there with heavy equipment to catch the leaf litter and other organic debris that are part of a healthy, naturally abundant river system.

Shinglemill Creek flowing on tidal marsh into Colvos Passage at low tide, Fern Cove Sanctuary, Vashon Island

Autumn leaves of bigleaf maple cover the black boulders of Fossil Creek, Mount Baker–Snoqualmie National Forest

Even in driest eastern Washington, wetlands refresh the landscape.

Wetlands cover just 2 percent of Washington's landmass, or 938,000 acres. They can be fresh water or salt water. Many are on the edge of a river or lake, a shallow pond or swamp, a marshy field or forested bog, or shrubby area bristling with willows. Others are isolated.

Wetlands lessen flooding by slowing runoff. They maintain stream flows by gradually releasing stored water after floods and rainy seasons. They also boost water quality by allowing runoff to filter through vegetation, so sediment is trapped. Nutrients and pollutants are also absorbed. Groundwater is recharged by water that seeps through roots and mud, purifying it as it percolates into the aquifer.

Shorelines are stabilized by wetlands, which diffuse the erosive power of waves and currents. Wetland plants hold the soil with their roots, creating a natural buffer that absorbs the water's energy.

Wetlands also provide important habitats to nearly five hundred species of animals across the state. Some animals, like beavers, spend their entire lives in wetlands, while others, including salmon and shorebirds, depend on wetlands during their migration.

Wetland preservation is an uphill battle. More than a third of Washington's wetlands have been lost since European settlement. In some parts of the populous Puget Sound region, more than 90 percent of the wetlands have been destroyed.

LOWER GRAND COULEE

Lower Grand Coulee is part of more than 250 square miles of cliffs and scablands carved by ancient floods in eastern Washington. Water, the master sculptor, has left its mark here in a long parade of ancient lake and river beds, linked through miles of water-carved basalt.

The Grand Coulee is a fifty-mile-long trench ranging from one to six miles wide, with steep walls of basalt up to nine hundred feet high. These massive, chiseled waterways are softened by wildflowers, tall grasses, and a soft silence that graces this largely unpeopled part of the state.

In the Lower Grand Coulee, there are four peaceful lakes in a string. Lenore Lake is the largest, filling a six-mile-long scoured-out depression in the basalt. The western wall above the lake towers more than eight hundred feet high.

There is both majesty and delicacy to this landscape of craggy, sheer rock walls, still water, and soft, bright wildflowers. Close your eyes here and listen; all you will hear is the wind rushing through canyons, the rustle of dry grass, the call of waterfowl, and the sound of your own breathing.

opposite page
Red-osier dogwood and cattails along the shores of Forde Lake, Sinlahekin Wildlife Area

below
An entangled mass of common sunflowers along the banks of Lenore Lake in the basin of the Lower Grand Coulee, North Columbia Basin Wildlife Refuge

It is hard to believe this river, more than three hundred miles from the Pacific in the far southeastern corner of Washington, is home to salmon. But, like the Snake and the mighty Columbia, the Grande Ronde is crucial to these fantastic fish.

When the salmon reach these freshwater rivers of their birth, they are in the final stage of their life cycle. After anywhere from two, three, four, or more years in the ocean, they return to fresh water. They stop eating once they leave salt water and move with ruthless focus, stopping only when they reach their birthplace. There they spawn and die, and their bodies help nourish the next generation of these noble fish.

The miracle of the salmon's migration seems clearest here, worlds apart from the sea on the high bare hills of the Grande Ronde. It is a surprise even to see a river—or water at all—in this arid inland place, known for dryland wheat fields, grain elevators, and open sky.

Evening light on patterned ridges above the winding Grande Ronde River, Asotin County

Vine maple at cedar forest edge above the North Fork of Granite Creek, Kaniksu National Forest

The Northwest, for some, is defined as wherever the salmon run.

Throughout Washington, hundreds of clear, cold, fast streams nurture silvery runs of salmon. These fish travel from their native stream to the ocean and back. They require a range of pristine habitats from fresh water to salt, and are an indicator species for the state. Where the salmon thrive, all is as it should be.

The gravel beds of the creeks are clean and deep. Streams meander their natural course, with back eddies and side channels that provide places for salmon to rest and feed. Woody debris on the stream bottom slows the flow, but a swift current runs in the main channel, flushing young salmon, called smolts, to the sea.

Diversions of water for irrigation rob streams of their flow. Logging strips the banks and headwaters of trees that hold the soil in place, resulting in flooding that tears out stream banks and scours the bottom clean of the gravel that is essential for sheltering salmon eggs.

Puget Sound chinook, long one of Washington's most prized salmon, were listed for protection in March 1999, by the federal government under the Endangered Species Act. It's a wake-up call that must be acted on to restore and preserve the habitat the salmon depend on, for we depend on it, too.

North Fork of the Skokomish River flowing around red reef limestone at Staircase Rapids, Olympic National Park

Of all the gifts water brings to Washington State, its artistry is among the most precious.

On summer mornings, the dew makes even the most common things, from farm fences to uncut grass, into supports for sparkling spider sculpture. Here, the morning light backlights constellations of dewdrops snared in the spiders' silvery webs.

It is amazing how much dew their webs can carry; some span across wide distances, but still do not tear. The dew is a product of Washington's cool summer nights. Water droplets settle out of the air as it cools, leaving a heavy blanket of dew on everything.

An ordinary lawn becomes a pavement of tiny diamonds, and feet leave tracks in the grass. Walk the dog in a tallgrass meadow, and pants become soaked to the knee.

That's okay. It's worth it to enjoy this wet, dewy elixir of summer.

Spider web patterns with dew drops in morning light, Vashon Island

CHAPTER 5

SPIRIT

Blue-pod lupine intermixes with grasses on Steptoe Butte
with the green hills of the Palouse country in the
distance, Steptoe Butte State Park

THE SPIRIT OF wild nature abides in Washington's landscapes. There can be danger in some of these places, and even more danger in not going there.

We need these places. They soothe a sad and lonely heart, inspire awe, and reconnect us to our better selves. They remind us of forces of nature and measures of time far bigger than our crabbed and petty worries.

There are wildlands still big and pristine enough to be home to the lynx, the grizzly bear, and the bald eagle.

There are more glaciers than in any other state but Alaska, and mountains steeper than the Rockies.

There are glacial meltwater streams that will make your teeth ache; rivers furious with white water and studded with rocks hauled there by the claws of glaciers in the last Ice Age.

The vast and wild Pacific rages in winter storms and tosses old-growth logs like bathtub toys.

In the sagebrush country there are still open spaces big enough to get lost in, lost long enough to worry about it.

The long light of late afternoon plays across outdoor sculpture gardens of ancient basalt rock. Birdsong is as it's meant to be heard, uninterrupted by the noise of people, and carrying in full, bright voice across vast, open space.

There are places with quiet so deep it has dimension, and night skies so dark every star burns bright.

A sense of things wild and free lives on in Washington's wildlands. These landscapes connect us back to the essential elements of nature, and to the spirit of the land.

Morning light on snow-covered peaks of Johannesburg Mountain, from the Cascade River canyon, North Cascades National Park

The Willapa National Wildlife Refuge, in the southwest corner of Washington above the mouth of the Columbia, is a sanctuary of quiet, made musical by tall marsh grasses and the lap of the tide. The refuge includes 11,500 acres of uplands and tidelands around Willapa Bay, one of the cleanest, most productive coastal ecosystems remaining in the continental United States.

The saltwater wetlands of the Willapa perform a vital, water-cleansing function: filtering the runoff of streams tumbling into the salt water from the forested uplands. The salt marsh grasses grow at the mouths of the larger rivers, within reach of the tidewater.

Great gyres of migration and cycles of the tide are the timekeepers here.

Marsh grasses braided by the wind and receding tides on Willapa Bay, Willapa National Wildlife Refuge

A Totem Mountain

Mount Rainier is an icon of Washington as potent as the salmon.

Native Americans wove Rainier into many myths, often casting the mountain in the role of wife of neighboring peaks. In some myths, the top of Mount Rainier was a dwelling place of powerful spirits. The Nisqually, who established their villages in the watershed Rainier crowns, believed that if there was any one place where the Great Creator rested on earth, it was the summit of Mount Rainier.

Pink sky at dawn from Upper Tipsoo Lake reflecting Mount Rainier in its just-starting-to-freeze surface in early winter, Mount Rainier National Park

In winter, the artistry of frost on the grass and brilliance of snow and ice on the landscape can take your breath away.

Snow and frost are rare enough for flatlanders on the West Side that they are cause to stop everything, go out for a walk, and savor the brilliant landscape.

I've watched my black Labrador Molly run through crystallized tall grass in an abandoned orchard near our house, plowing up powdery white frost with her fine black snout. Then she will snort gleefully, sending the white crystals flying and glittering in the sun.

The clean, sparkling land is pure refreshment for both of us.

Morning sun on frosted maple and alder trees along the frozen North Fork of the Nooksack River, Mount Baker–Snoqualmie National Forest

Frosty grasses encircling stream reflection of Liberty Bell Mountain, Washington Meadows at Washington Pass, Okanogan National Forest

Fall-colored grasses and western larch
under Prusik Peak, Enchantment Lakes,
Alpine Lakes Wilderness Area,
Wenatchee National Forest

Touch the earth, love the earth, honor the earth, her plains, her valleys, her hills and seas. Rest your spirit in the solitary places."
—*Henry Beston,* The Outermost House, *1949*

The music of water refreshes the spirit as much as the land.

Sound recordist Bernie Krause has spent most of his life collecting the sounds of nature, all over the world. He believes we need to hear the sounds of nature as much as we need to breathe clean air.

Krause believes we live in a visual culture. He says we have forgotten how to hear. It comes at a price—of peace, of knowing ourselves and where we come from.

We need deep drinks of what he calls "ancient sounds" of birds, bugs, bees, wind, rain, waves, and rushing streams. We need to hear what Krause calls the "biophony of nature," the symphony of a healthy, diverse habitat.

"The natural world offers a safer harbor than anything we might have imagined," Krause says. "It's the only innocent place left.

"We can each come to know a little of this fabulous realm, and find our own path to it."

White water rushes over boulders in the North Fork of the Nooksack River, Mount Baker–Snoqualmie National Forest

Evening light on basalt boulder with yarrow and grasses, Drumheller Channels National Natural Landmark, Columbia National Wildlife Refuge

The snowy white surprise of yarrow, with its delicate fernlike leaves, is a gift of grace amid the rugged beauty of the scablands. This country is a land of contrasts, of delicate wildflowers and rocky terrain. It bakes in the summer, and freezes solid in the winter. Yet, wildflowers and tiny lichen manage in this harsh climate. Yarrow thrives.

The whole plant is woolly and fragrant and has a long history of medicinal uses. Its finely cut leaves are steeped in tea that some believe cures everything from an unhappy love life to baldness. The leaves are also applied as a poultice to stop bleeding. *Achillea millefolium* loves fields and roadsides, and stands one to three feet tall. Its flat-topped flowers grace open, sunny meadows in summer.

Yarrow still heals today, offering quiet solace for the soul.

Water and Sky

Here in the far Northeast corner of the state, hard by the Canadian border, fall comes earlier, and the colors seem to burn brighter under the crystalline clear skies of eastern Washington.

In this peaceful landscape the stillness of the water can be so absolute the reflection of the clouds is mirror bright. You could mistake the water for the sky, but for the golden larch needles floating in lazy patterns.

Fall colors of western larch reflect along the shore of Frater Lake, Colville National Forest

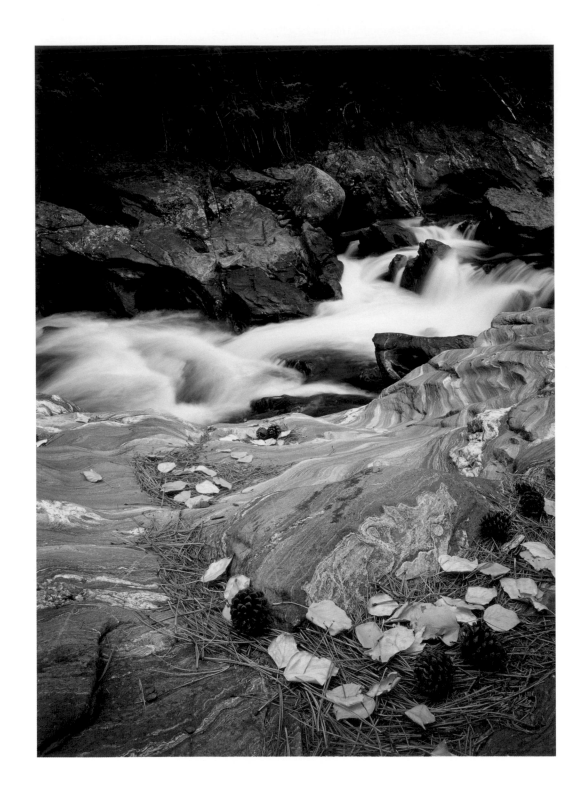

Beauty on a Small Scale

Black cottonwood leaves, pine needles, and cones on water-worn rock of the Icicle River Gorge, Wenatchee National Forest

Washington's beauty can be grand and sweeping, or intimate as a poem, inviting contemplation. It takes time to see the loveliness that nature makes in the smaller places, to see the perfect composition in nature's form. Though this beauty is spare, it is complete, a visual haiku.

THOUSANDS OF TIRED, nerve-shaken, over-civilized people are beginning to find out that going to the mountains is going home; the wildness is a necessity. . . ."

—*John Muir, "The Wild Parks and Reservations of the West," 1898*

Bowan Mountain with sunset clouds and moon rise from the South Fork of Bridge Creek, North Cascades National Park

The camas flower, a member of the lily family, was an important staple for Native peoples who gathered the roots for their basic starch food.

The roots can be eaten any number of ways: fresh, dried, baked, boiled, or pounded to a meal.

The plant's common name is derived from a word which means "sweet" in the language of the Nootka, a tribe on Vancouver Island. It tastes like a cross between maple sugar and brown sugar.

Gathering and baking the roots in a pit of hot embers was an important community ceremony, a timeless ritual of taking sustenance from the land and sharing it as a people.

Camas roots provide nourishment still, fueling limpid pools of blue flowers that feed the spirit.

"PROSPECTUS FOR VISITORS"

The intimacy of a mist-cloaked horizon brings the heroic landscape of Mount Rainier National Park to a more human scale. Flowers smolder in the gray. The muffled, upholstered atmosphere makes the quiet deep and velvety.

This gray is penetrating, insinuating. Vern Rutsala, a Northwest poet, warns of the Northwest's infamous gloom in his poem, "Prospectus for Visitors":

> You should know as well
> that all this rich green
> always loses to the gray.
>
> Even the winter roses
> fade, even the camellias
> fail—or seem to under
> that sky.
>
> It's the low
> sky that's always there,
> that knitted cap. If
> you want to stay
> learn to wear it
> from October on. . . .

opposite page
Field of common camas and buttercup in Catherine Creek Natural Area, Columbia River Gorge National Scenic Area

below
Pink mountain heather, lupine, and giant red paintbrush blooming alongside boulders in Paradise Park, Mount Rainier National Park

Washington's rivers are a reminder of the connections between the uplands and the low, the mountains and the sea, and between us all. The rivers murmur wise counsel: We all live downstream.

Our lives are bound with water, and no one seemed to understand this as well as the First People, who depended on healthy salmon runs for survival.

They believed these noble fish traveled in two worlds: the river, and a spirit world under the sea, where the salmon would dwell in houses, like people.

Many Washington tribes practiced a ceremony of the first salmon, and some still do today. The first salmon caught of the year was carefully cooked and shared among The People. Then its bones were returned with reverence to the river, its backbone carefully kept intact.

If treated with respect, it was hoped the salmon would return. Caretaking of the salmon's habitat and sustainable harvest was our part of the bargain. It still is.

Stream violet and false Solomon's seal bordering a creek in the Upper Sol Duc River valley, Olympic National Park

L IKE WINDS AND sunsets, wild things were taken for granted until progress began to do away with them. Now we face the question whether a still higher 'standard of living' is worth its cost in things natural, wild and free. For us in the minority, the opportunity to see geese is more important than television, and the chance to find a pasque-flower is a right as inalienable as free speech."
—*Aldo Leopold,* A Sand County Almanac, and Sketches Here and There, *1949*

The waters of the Paradise River flow over granite boulders through a fir and spruce forest, Mount Rainier National Park

I WENT TO THE woods because I wished to live deliberately, to front only the essential facts of life, and see if I could not learn what it had to teach, and not, when I came to die, discover that I had not lived."

—*Henry David Thoreau,* Walden, *1854*

above
Heavy snow in forest of Douglas fir and western red cedar near Denny Creek, Mount Baker–Snoqualmie National Forest

right
Willows, alders, and vine maples reflecting on the calm surface of Monte Cristo Lake, Mount Baker–Snoqualmie National Forest

CONCLUSION

NATIVE AMERICAN TRIBES living along the Columbia River carved these prehistoric petroglyphs.

We have much to learn from these people who lived so long, and so lightly, on the earth. Today our numbers and needs are bigger than those of these early hunter-gatherer societies. But nature sustains us today as much as it ever did. We may, in fact, need wild nature even more as our day-to-day lives become more disconnected from the land.

We need ecosystems that are intact and healthy. We need them not only in parks, but also in our day-to-day lives. Parks are essential, but so are the landscapes we live in and among. Nature is not something to be visited, like a zoo.

These petroglyphs teach us that people have lived in Washington's landscapes for thousands of years. And still the spirit of the land perseveres. These landscapes are a priceless inheritance, but to receive their gifts, the land must be respected. Its gifts come with a duty of caretaking, so that generations to come may also be nurtured by the spirit of the land.

Petroglyphs on basalt from the
Columbia River Gorge

BIBLIOGRAPHY

T HERE IS A wealth of information available on the wonderfully complex ecology, geology, and botany of Washington's landscapes. The following are books I relied on in compiling the text. All of these books would be rewarding further reading for anyone wanting to learn more about this fabulous land.

Allen, John Eliot, Marjorie Burns, and Sam C. Sargent. *Cataclysms on the Columbia.* Portland, Ore.: Timber Press, 1986. For information about the Channeled Scablands and the Spokane Flood.

Alt, David D., and Donald W. Hyndman. *Roadside Geology of Washington.* Missoula, Mont.: Mountain Press Publishing Company, 1984.

Alt, David D., and Donald W. Hyndman. *Northwest Exposures: A Geologic Story of the Northwest.* Missoula, Mont.: Mountain Press, 1995.

Barcott, Bruce. *The Measure of a Mountain: Beauty and Terror on Mount Rainier.* Seattle: Sasquatch Books, 1997. A book full of love for The Mountain, funny accounts of Barcott's efforts to understand and finally climb it, as well as reams of factual data about Mount Rainier.

Brill, Steve, with Evelyn Dean. *Identifying and Harvesting Edible and Medicinal Plants in Wild (and Not So Wild) Places.* New York: Hearst Books, 1994.

Clark, Ella E. *Indian Legends of the Pacific Northwest.* Berkeley: University of California Press, 1953.

Hanify, Mary Lou, and Craig Blencowe. *Guide to the Hoh Rain Forest.* Seattle: Pacific Northwest Parks Association, 1974.

Harris, Ann G., and Esther Tuttle, with Sherwood D. Tuttle. *Geology of National Parks*, 5th ed. Dubuque, Iowa: Kendall/Hunt Publishing Company, 1997.

Harris, Jim. "My Place in the Mountains." In *Impressions of the North Cascades: Essays About a Northwest Landscape,* edited by John C. Miles. Seattle: The Mountaineers, 1996. This fine book offers many perspectives on a fantastic landscape, from the geologic to the poetic. I am indebted to Jim Harris's lovely essay for the idea that preserving our day-to-day landscapes in addition to our parks is important.

Kirk, Ruth, with Jerry Franklin. *The Olympic Rain Forest: An Ecological Web.* Seattle: University of Washington Press, 1992.

Krause, Bernie. *Into a Wild Sanctuary: A Life in Music & Natural Sound.* Berkeley, Calif.: Heydey Books, 1998.

Laskin, David. *Rains all the Time: A Connoisseur's History of Weather in the Pacific Northwest.* Seattle: Sasquatch Books, 1997. I relied on this wonderful book for weather statistics and recommend it to anyone wishing to explore the pathos of Washington's weather.

Leopold, Aldo. *A Sand County Almanac, and Sketches Here and There.* New York:

Oxford University Press, 1949.

McMillan, Bruce. *The Weather Sky.* New York: Farrar, Straus & Giroux, 1991.

McNulty, Tim, and Pat O'Hara. *Washington's Wild Rivers: The Unfinished Work.* Seattle: The Mountaineers, 1990.

Meany, Edmond S. *Vancouver's Discovery of Puget Sound.* Portland, Ore.: Binfords & Mort, 1949.

Muir, John. *John Muir In His Own Words.* Edited by Peter Browning. Lafayette, Calif.: Great West Books, 1988.

Murphey, Edith van Allen. *Indian Uses of Native Plants.* Glenwood, Ill.: Meyerbooks, 1958.

Newton, James R. *Rain Shadow.* New York: Thomas R. Crowell, 1983. A children's book that I often re-read to get a reality check in relation to the books written for adults!

Palmer, Tim. *The Snake River: Window to the West.* Washington, D.C.: Island Press, 1991. This definitive work—with photographs by the author—offers anything you'd want to know about the Snake.

Peattie, Donald Culross. *A Natural History of Western Trees.* Boston: Houghton Mifflin, 1953. This delightful book elevates the field guide to a fine art. Ebullient writing and vivid descriptions throughout celebrate every tree in the west. This is a book to read front to back for the sheer pleasure of it.

Rapp, Valerie. *What the River Reveals: Understanding and Restoring Healthy Watersheds.* Seattle: The Mountaineers, 1997.

Ross, Robert A., and Henrietta L. Chambers. *Wildflowers of the Western Cascades.* Portland, Ore.: Timber Press, 1988.

Rutsala, Vern. "Prospectus for Visitors." In *Selected Poems.* Brownsville, Ore.: Story Line Press, 1991. This poem is a treasure, and I would recommend tracking down the original (only a few stanzas appear in this book) to anyone who seeks to better understand living in the Northwest climate.

Stewart, Charles. *Wildflowers of the Olympics and Cascades.* 2nd ed. Port Angeles, Wash.: Nature Education Enterprises, 1994.

Taylor, Ronald J. *Sagebrush Country: A Wildflower Sanctuary.* Missoula, Mont.: Mountain Press Publishing Company, 1992.

Tilford, Gregory L. *Edible and Medicinal Plants of the West.* Missoula, Mont.: Mountain Press, 1997.

Turner, Nancy J. *Food Plants of Coastal First Peoples.* Seattle: University of Washington Press, 1995.

Weis, Paul L., and William L. Newman, eds. *The Channeled Scablands of Eastern Washington: The Geologic Story of the Spokane Flood.* Cheney, Wash.: Eastern Washington University Press, 1989.

Weisberg, Saul, and Jon Riedel. *From the Mountains to the Sea: A Guide to the Skagit River Watershed.* Sedro Woolley, Wash.: North Cascades Institute, 1991. A little book that packs a lot of information about the mountains, rivers, wildlife, and history of the Skagit River watershed.

Whitney, Stephen. *Western Forests.* Audubon Society Nature Guides. New York: Alfred A. Knopf, 1985.

Wolf, Edward C. *A Tidewater Place: Portrait of the Willapa Ecosystem.* Long Beach, Wash.: The Willapa Alliance, in cooperation with the Nature Conservancy and Ecotrust, 1993. This slim book is full of information about this lovely place, and the photographs are gorgeous.

PHOTO CREDITS

Page 1 © Terry Donnelly

Pages 2–3 © Terry Donnelly

Page 5 © Terry Donnelly

Page 6 © Terry Donnelly

Pages 8–9 © Mary Liz Austin

Page 11 © Terry Donnelly

Page 13 © Terry Donnelly

Page 14 © Terry Donnelly

Page 15 © Terry Donnelly

Page 16 © Terry Donnelly

Page 17 © Mary Liz Austin

Pages 18–19 © Terry Donnelly

Page 21 © Mary Liz Austin

Page 22 © Mary Liz Austin

Page 23 © Terry Donnelly

Page 24 © Mary Liz Austin

Page 25 © Terry Donnelly

Page 26 © Terry Donnelly

Page 27 © Terry Donnelly

Page 28 © Terry Donnelly

Page 29 © Mary Liz Austin

Page 31 © Terry Donnelly

Page 32 © Terry Donnelly

Page 33 © Terry Donnelly

Page 34 (inset) © Terry Donnelly

Pages 34–35 © Terry Donnelly

Page 36 © Terry Donnelly

Page 37 © Terry Donnelly

Page 38 © Terry Donnelly

Page 39 © Mary Liz Austin

Pages 40–41 © Terry Donnelly

Pages 42–43 © Mary Liz Austin

Page 45 © Terry Donnelly

Page 46 (inset) © Terry Donnelly

Pages 46–47 © Mary Liz Austin

Page 48 © Mary Liz Austin

Page 49 © Terry Donnelly

Page 50 © Terry Donnelly

Page 51 © Terry Donnelly

Page 52 © Terry Donnelly

Page 53 © Mary Liz Austin

Page 54 © Terry Donnelly

Page 55 © Mary Liz Austin

Page 56 © Terry Donnelly

Page 57 © Terry Donnelly

Page 58 © Terry Donnelly

Page 59 © Terry Donnelly

Page 60 © Terry Donnelly

Page 61 © Terry Donnelly

Pages 62–63 © Terry Donnelly

Page 65 © Terry Donnelly

Page 66 © Mary Liz Austin

Page 67 © Mary Liz Austin

Page 68 © Terry Donnelly

Page 69 © Terry Donnelly

Pages 70–71 © Terry Donnelly

Page 72 © Terry Donnelly

Page 73 © Terry Donnelly

Page 74 © Terry Donnelly

Page 75 © Terry Donnelly

Page 76 © Terry Donnelly

Page 77 © Mary Liz Austin

Page 78 © Terry Donnelly

Page 80 © Terry Donnelly

Page 81 © Terry Donnelly

Page 83 © Mary Liz Austin

Page 84 © Terry Donnelly

Page 86 © Terry Donnelly

Page 87 © Terry Donnelly

Pages 88–89 © Mary Liz Austin

Pages 90–91 © Terry Donnelly

Page 93 © Terry Donnelly

Page 94 © Terry Donnelly

Page 95 © Terry Donnelly

Page 96 © Terry Donnelly

Page 97 © Terry Donnelly

Page 98 © Terry Donnelly

Page 99 (top) © Mary Liz Austin

Page 99 (bottom) © Terry Donnelly

Page 101 © Terry Donnelly

Page 102 © Terry Donnelly

Page 103 © Terry Donnelly

Page 104 © Terry Donnelly

Page 105 © Terry Donnelly

Pages 106–107 © Terry Donnelly

Page 108 © Terry Donnelly

Page 109 © Mary Liz Austin

Page 110 © Terry Donnelly

Page 111 © Mary Liz Austin

Pages 112–113 © Terry Donnelly

Page 114 © Terry Donnelly

Page 115 © Terry Donnelly

Page 117 © Terry Donnelly

Pages 118–119 © Mary Liz Austin

Page 121 © Terry Donnelly

Page 122 © Mary Liz Austin

Page 123 © Mary Liz Austin

Page 124 © Terry Donnelly

Page 125 © Terry Donnelly

Page 126 © Terry Donnelly

Page 127 © Mary Liz Austin

Page 128 © Mary Liz Austin

Page 129 © Terry Donnelly

Page 130 © Terry Donnelly

Page 131 © Mary Liz Austin

Page 132 © Mary Liz Austin

Page 133 © Terry Donnelly

Page 134 © Terry Donnelly

Page 135 © Terry Donnelly

Page 136 (inset) © Terry Donnelly

Pages 136–137 © Terry Donnelly

Page 139 © Terry Donnelly

ABOUT THE AUTHOR AND PHOTOGRAPHERS

Photograph © Kathleen Webster

Author Lynda Mapes is a reporter for the *Seattle Times*, covering regional, natural resource, and environmental issues. She was a reporter at the *Spokane Spokesman Review*, covering the Washington State Legislature, statewide political stories, and news in Seattle and western Washington from bureaus in Olympia and Seattle. She won national and regional awards for a special series investigating salmon recovery efforts in the Pacific Northwest. Mapes lives on Vashon Island in Puget Sound with her husband Zack Krieger.

Photograph © Kathleen Webster

Over the past decade, photographers Terry Donnelly and Mary Liz Austin have traveled extensively throughout North America photographing national parks, public lands, popular travel destinations, and the American countryside. In their work, they seek those elusive conditions that reveal the mystery and grandeur of nature. Their images appear in numerous magazines, including *Sierra, Audubon,* and *Outside,* as well as in books and calendars published by National Geographic Books, Reiman Publications, BrownTrout, and Voyageur Press. Abbeville Press published their first book, *Heaven on Earth,* in 1999. Donnelly and Austin also make their home on Vashon Island.